A Visit to EGYPT

Peter and Connie Roop

Heinemann
LIBRARY

First published in Great Britain by Heinemann Library
Halley Court, Jordan Hill, Oxford OX2 8EJ
a division of Reed Educational and Professional Publishing Ltd.
Heinemann is a registered trademark of Reed Educational & Professional Publishing Limited.

OXFORD MELBOURNE AUCKLAND
IBADAN JOHANNESBURG GABORONE BLANTYRE
PORTSMOUTH (NH) USA CHICAGO

© Reed Educational and Professional Publishing Ltd 2000
The moral right of the proprietor has been asserted.

Designed by AMR and Celia Floyd
Illustrations by Art Construction
Colour Reproduction by Dot Gradations, U.K.
Printed and bound in Hong Kong/China

04 03 02 01 00
10 9 8 7 6 5 4 3 2 1

ISBN 0 431 08281 2

British Library Cataloguing in Publication Data

Roop, Peter
A visit to Egypt. – (Take-off!)
1. Egypt – Social conditions – 1952 – Juvenile literature
2. Egypt – Geography – Juvenile literature
3. Egypt – Social life and customs – 20th century – Juvenile literature
I. Title II. Roop, Connie III. Egypt
962'.055

Acknowledgements

The Publishers would like to thank the following for permission to reproduce photographs:
J Allan Cash: p20; Ian Cook: p24; Robert Harding Picture Library: F J Jackson p19, E Simanor p25; Hutchison Library: p22, S Errington p15, J Hart p14, Liba p28, Regent p8, L Taylor p23, B Wills p17; Christine Osborne Pictures: pp 7, 9, 12, 13, 18; Peter Sanders: p29; Spectrum Colour Library: p26; Trip: R Cracknell p6, E James pp 21, 27, P Mitchell p16, A Tovy p11; Zefa: p5, C Friere p10, Maroon p9.

Cover photograph reproduced with permission of Tony Stone/Doug Armand

Our thanks to Sue Graves for her advice and expertise in the preparation of this book.

Every effort has been made to contact holders of any material reproduced in this book. Any omissions will be rectified in subsequent printings if notice is given to the Publisher.

For more information about Heinemann Library books, or to order, please telephone +44 (0)1865 888066, or send a fax to +44 (0)1865 314091. You can visit our website at www.heinemann.co.uk

Any words appearing in bold, **like this**, are explained in the Glossary.

Contents

Egypt

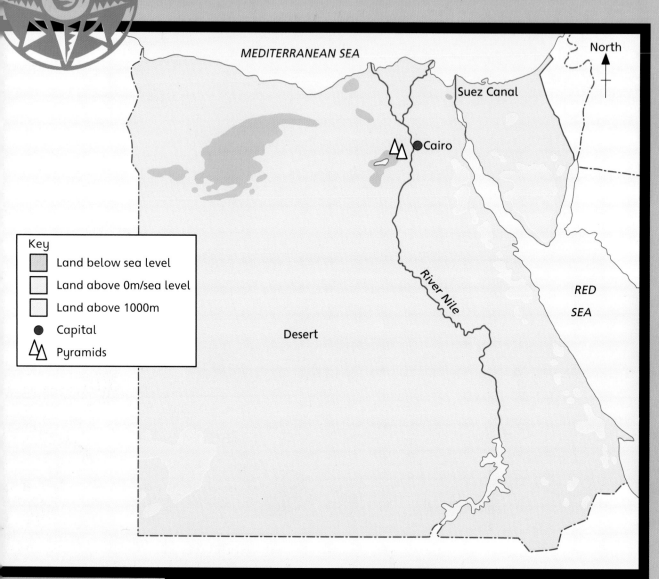

MEDITERRANEAN SEA

North

Suez Canal

Cairo

Key
- Land below sea level
- Land above 0m/sea level
- Land above 1000m
- Capital
- Pyramids

River Nile

RED SEA

Desert

Egypt is shaped like a square.

Egypt is in the north-east corner of Africa. The Mediterranean Sea lies off its north coast. The Red Sea lies off its east coast.

pyramid

Sphinx

The Sphinx stands near to the pyramids.

Many people visit Egypt to see the **ancient** buildings. More than 2000 years ago the Egyptians built **temples**, the **pyramids** and the **Sphinx**.

Land

There are many mountains in Egypt.

Egypt is a hot, dry country. Mountains and **desert** cover most of Egypt. The desert is the Sahara Desert. The longest river in the world flows through Egypt. It is called the River Nile.

The Sahara Desert is the biggest desert in the world.

crops

water pump

The land by the River Nile is good for growing crops.

Egyptians have lived along the River Nile for 5000 years. Today, nine out of every ten Egyptians still live near there. They live near the River Nile because the land is good for growing **crops**.

7

Landmarks

minaret →

River Nile

Cairo lies on the banks of the River Nile.

Cairo is the **capital** of Egypt. It is also the largest city in Egypt and Africa. About 7 million people live there. In Cairo you can see **mosques** with tall towers on the top called **minarets**.

8

Pyramids were the tombs of dead Pharaohs.

The Egyptians built the **pyramids** for their kings, called Pharaohs. They put the body of the dead Pharaoh inside the pyramid. The pyramids were built with large blocks of stone.

The blocks of stone weigh up to 15 tonnes each!

Homes

People live in flats above this restaurant.

The crowded Egyptian cities have old and new buildings. Most people live in small houses or flats.

These Bedouin people live in the desert.

In the country, homes are made of sun-dried bricks. In the **desert**, people live in tents. **Bedouin** people live in the desert. They are always moving their tents to find food and water for their animals.

Food

This man is cooking food, in the street, to sell.

Egyptians usually eat five small meals a day. They eat some food on the way to work or school. Food **stalls** sell snacks including rice, lamb and olives.

This boy is buying a dish of ful from a food stall.

Egyptians eat ful everyday. Ful is a special mixture of spices, beans and tomatoes. Sweet pastries called havla and baklava are favourite snacks.

Clothes

galabiyah

Egyptian men wear loose-fitting, long clothes.

Egyptians have many kinds of clothes. Some Egyptian men like to wear cotton trousers and a long shirt called a galabiyah.

These Egyptian women like to wear brightly coloured clothes.

Some Egyptian women wear a black dress, like a galabiyah. Many Egyptian women and children dress in bright colours. These women keep their heads covered, too.

Work

These farmers are working on their land next to the River Nile.

Many people are farmers in Egypt. They farm the land on the banks of the River Nile. They grow **crops** like vegetables, corn, sugar cane, cotton, rice, figs, grapes and dates.

Oil is an important Egyptian **export**.

Other people work with cotton, steel and oil
products. These are important to Egypt because
they can be sold to other countries.

Transport

felucca

People sail feluccas on the River Nile.

Not many Egyptian people have cars. Most of them walk or travel by bus or train. They use boats called feluccas on the River Nile.

Suez Canal

Big ships use the Suez Canal to save time.

Egypt has a very important channel for ships. It is
called the Suez **Canal**. Big ships take a short cut
through the Suez Canal. This saves them from
sailing all the way around Africa.

Find the Suez Canal on the map on page 4.

19

Language

These Egyptians speak to each other in Arabic.

Egypt's national language is Arabic. People also speak Greek, Italian, English and French.

120 million people speak Arabic in North Africa and the Middle East.

A modern Arabic language is being created in Egypt.

Egyptians speak nine kinds of Arabic. Now Egyptians are creating one modern Arabic language. Soon they will all be able to understand each other.

School

Egyptian school children.

All Egyptian children between the ages of 6 and 14 must go to school. Children learn maths, reading, science, music, French, English and art.

These children write Arabic from right to left across the page.

Egyptian children learn to read and write Arabic. Arabic has 28 letters. You read it from right to left.

Free time

People swim in the River Nile on hot days.

Football (soccer) is a favourite Egyptian sport. People also play basketball, tennis, **squash** and volleyball. On hot days they swim in the River Nile to cool off.

This souk is a busy place.

Egyptians enjoy spending time at the souk. A souk is an outdoor market with many **stalls**. The stalls have lots of fresh food such as vegetables and fruit.

Celebrations

Music is played at Egyptian weddings.

In Egypt, families celebrate many special occasions together. Weddings are a time for dressing up in best clothes, eating good food and dancing to music.

Muslims like to celebrate the end of Ramadan.

Ramadan is the most important celebration for **Muslims**. People pray and **fast** for a month. Families get together to celebrate at the end of it.

The Arts

Music is important to Egyptians.

Films are very popular in Egypt. Many films are made in Cairo. Egyptians are also a musical people. They play their music on **lutes**, drums and tambourines.

Reading is important to Egyptians.

Egyptians also enjoy reading. In 1988, an Egyptian writer named Naguib Mahfouz won the prize for the world's best writing.

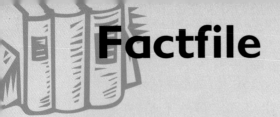

Factfile

Name   The full name of Egypt is the Arab Republic of Egypt.

Capital   The **capital** city is Cairo.

Language   Most Egyptians speak Arabic.

Population There are more than 56 million people living in Egypt.

Money   Instead of the dollar or the pound, the Egyptians have the Egyptian pound.

Religions   Most Egyptian people believe in **Islam** or Christianity.

Products   Egypt produces lots of oil, cotton, fruits and vegetables.

Words you can learn

ahlan wa sahlan	hello
ma'as salama	goodbye
ismi	My name is
shukran	thank you
aywa	yes
la'	no
waHid	one
itnein	two
talata	three

Glossary

ancient	from a long time ago
Bedouin	a group of people who live in tents in the desert
canal	river dug by people
capital	the city where the government is based
crops	the plants that farmers grow
desert	large areas of land that have little or no rain and very few plants or animals
export	goods sold to another country
fast	to go without anything to eat or drink
Islam	the main religion of Egypt
lute	a musical instrument like a guitar
minaret	a tower at the top of a mosque. A minaret is used to call people to prayer
mosque	a place of worship for Muslims
Muslims	people who believe in the Islamic religion
products	things which are grown, taken from the earth, made by hand or made in a factory
pyramids	the enormous stone buildings in the desert that have triangular sides
Sphinx	the huge stone sculpture built next to the pyramids, it has the body of a lion and the head of a human
squash	a game played with a racket and a hard ball
stalls	tables and shelves laid out with things for sale
temples	buildings used as places of worship

Index